THE
IRISH
PUB

Fabulous food from the Emerald Isle

First published in 2012

Love Food ® is an imprint of Parragon Books Ltd

Parragon
Queen Street House
4 Queen Street
Bath BA1 1HE, UK

www.parragon.com/lovefood

ISBN: 978-1-4454-7396-3

Printed in China

Recipes by Christine McFadden
Home economy by Lincoln Jefferson
Photography by Mike Cooper

Notes for the Reader
This book uses standard kitchen measuring spoons and cups. All spoon and cup measurements are level unless otherwise indicated. Unless otherwise stated, milk is assumed to be whole, eggs are large, individual vegetables are medium, and pepper is freshly ground black pepper.

The times given are only an approximate guide. Preparation times differ according to the techniques used by different people and the cooking times may also vary from those given. Optional ingredients, variations, or serving suggestions have not been included in the calculations.

Recipes using raw or very lightly cooked eggs should be avoided by infants, the elderly, pregnant women, convalescents, and anyone with a chronic illness. Pregnant and breast-feeding women are advised to avoid eating peanuts and peanut products. People with nut allergies should be aware that some of the prepared ingredients used in the recipes in this book may contain nuts. Always check the packaging before use.

Picture acknowledgments
The publisher would like to thank Getty Images for permission to reproduce copyright material: front cover Louis-Laurent Grandadam; 7 Altrendo travel; 9 Douglas Pearson; 24 David Cordner; 31 Design Pics / The Irish Image Collection; 53 Andy Goss; 60 & 65 IIC / Axiom; 75 Neale Clarke; 93 Ed Freeman

Contents

	Introduction	6
Chapter 1	Appetizers & Snacks	8
Chapter 2	Entrées	30
Chapter 3	Vegetables & Sides	52
Chapter 4	Desserts & Drinks	74
	Index	96

Introduction

Irish pubs come in all shapes and sizes. There are grand Victorian palaces in the big towns and cities, with ornate bars, wooden paneling, tiled floors, and stained-glass windows. In bustling market towns, they become the center of life on market days when deals are done and news is exchanged. Even tiny villages and hamlets will have their own pub, which may double-up as the local store, post office, or maybe the undertaker! Whatever their size or style, they are all great places to pull up a stool, sample a drink, and enjoy a chat.

As well as being the social center of their communities, many Irish pubs have also, in recent years, become great places to eat. A new generation of exciting young chefs has transformed Irish food, creating new dishes, and giving a twist to many of the classic favorites. Much of this is inspired by the fabulous local ingredients—rich dairy and subtle cheeses from the lush green pastureland; tender outdoor-raised meat; fresh fish and seafood from the long coastline and rivers; great-tasting vegetables from the fertile soil; and homely baked treats.

This collection brings together the best of the old and new. The Appetizers & Snacks chapter includes warming soups, fresh salads, and succulent seafood. For an Entrée, you could choose from the traditional Dublin Coddle or Cockle & Mussel Gratin, or treat your friends and family to a Michaelmas feast of roast goose. To accompany these are great ways to prepare the best of Irish vegetables—potatoes, cabbage, onions, and leeks, plus some easy and delicious breads. To round off your meal, try the Irish Whiskey Trifle or a taste-tingling Chocolate and Stout Ice Cream.

Whatever you choose, this book will bring you the true taste of some fabulous food from the Emerald Isle.

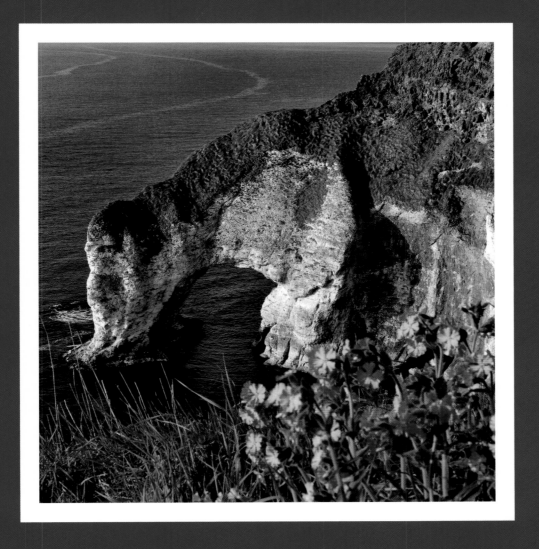

Chapter 1

APPETIZERS & SNACKS

Irish Buttermilk Pancakes

Nothing goes to waste in the Irish kitchen, including buttermilk—the thin liquid left over after churning butter. It has a pleasing, tangy flavor and is a main ingredient in Irish baking. Similar to drop biscuits in thickness, buttermilk pancakes have a slightly crisp, golden crust and a fluffy center.

Makes 12

1$^{1}/_{3}$ cups all-purpose flour
$^{3}/_{4}$ tablespoon sugar
$^{1}/_{2}$ teaspoon salt
1 teaspoon baking soda
1 egg, lightly beaten
1$^{1}/_{2}$ cups buttermilk
3 tablespoons vegetable oil, plus extra for brushing

To serve
$^{2}/_{3}$ cup heavy cream, whipped
1 cup blueberries

* Sift the flour, sugar, salt, and baking soda into a mixing bowl.

* Mix the egg with the buttermilk and vegetable oil in a large pitcher. Add to the dry ingredients, beating to a smooth, creamy batter. Let stand for at least 30 minutes or up to 2 hours.

* Heat a nonstick skillet or flat griddle pan over medium heat and brush with vegetable oil. Pour in enough batter to make 4-inch circles (about $^{1}/_{4}$ cup per pancake). Cook for 1$^{1}/_{2}$–2 minutes per side, or until small bubbles appear on the surface. Remove to a dish and keep warm while you cook the rest.

* Serve with softly whipped cream and blueberries.

Beef & Barley Broth

In Irish cuisine, instead of a clear soup or stock, broth refers to a hearty meal-in-a-bowl soup. Traditionally, the meat is cut up and divided among individual soup bowls before the broth is poured over. A floury potato for mopping up juices tops each bowl.

Serves 6

1½ pounds chuck steak
⅓ cup pearl barley, rinsed
⅓ cup green split peas, rinsed
1 large onion, thickly sliced
½ teaspoon black peppercorns
3 carrots, halved lengthwise and sliced
¾ cup diced rutabaga or turnip
1 small leek, some green tops included,
  thinly sliced
1 celery stalk, sliced
6 small floury potatoes, such as russets,
  white rounders, or Yukon gold, peeled
1½ cups sliced green cabbage
2 tablespoons chopped fresh parsley
salt

❖ Put the beef, pearl barley, and split peas in a large saucepan with the onion and peppercorns. Pour in enough cold water to just cover. Slowly bring to a boil, skimming off any foam, then reduce the heat, cover, and simmer gently for 1½ hours.

❖ Add the carrots, rutabaga, leek, and celery to the pan. Season with salt, and simmer for an additional 30 minutes. Add a little more water if the soup starts to look too thick.

❖ Meanwhile, put the potatoes in another saucepan with water to cover. Add salt to taste and bring to a boil. Cook for 7–10 minutes, until tender but not disintegrating. Drain, return to the pan, and cover with a clean dish towel.

❖ Remove the meat saucepan from the stove. Carefully lift out the meat using two forks or a slotted spoon. Cut into small cubes and return to the pan. Add the cabbage and simmer for an additional 5 minutes, or until the cabbage is just tender. Check the seasoning.

❖ Ladle the soup into warm wide soup bowls. Place a potato in the middle of each bowl and sprinkle with the parsley.

Scallop Chowder

Scallops are fished around the Irish coast, especially in winter and spring. With their dense flesh and delicately flavored corals, they are particularly good in creamy chowders, either on their own or mixed with other seafood. Be careful to avoid overcooking them, otherwise the flesh will become rubbery.

Serves 6

3½ tablespoons lightly salted butter
9 ounces large scallops, quartered
4 bacon strips, chopped
1 large onion, chopped
2 celery stalks, diced
2 carrots, diced
3 starchy potatoes, such as russets, white round, or Yukon gold, diced
2 fresh thyme sprigs
3 tablespoons chopped fresh parsley
2 cups chicken or vegetable stock
2 cups whole milk, scalded
9 ounces mixed cooked seafood, such as shrimp and mussels
squeeze of lemon juice
salt and pepper

- Melt the butter in a large saucepan over medium heat. When it sizzles, add the scallops and cook, in batches, for 5 minutes, until lightly colored. Remove from the pan and set aside.

- Add the bacon to the pan and cook for 3–4 minutes, until it starts to color.

- Add the onion, celery, carrots, and potatoes. Season with salt and pepper, then cover and cook over medium-low heat, stirring occasionally, until the vegetables start to soften.

- Add the thyme and 2 tablespoons of the parsley to the pan of vegetables. Pour in the stock, cover, and bring to a boil. Reduce the heat and simmer for 15 minutes, until the vegetables are soft.

- Remove and discard the thyme sprigs. Lightly crush some of the vegetables with a masher or the back of a wooden spoon to thicken the liquid. Pour in the scalded milk.

- Add the scallops and mixed seafood to the pan. Cook until heated through but without letting the mixture boil.

- Check the seasoning, and add a squeeze of lemon juice. Ladle into warm bowls and serve sprinkled with the remaining parsley.

Skink Soup

"Skink" is an old Irish and Scots term meaning "broth." This version, sometimes called Irish chicken soup, is made with diced chicken and colorful summer vegetables, enriched with cream and egg yolk. Although lighter than traditional winter broths, it still makes a satisfying meal-in-a-bowl.

Serves 4

2 celery stalks, halved lengthwise and diced
4 small carrots, thinly sliced
1 small leek, halved lengthwise and sliced
3$\frac{1}{2}$ cups chicken stock
1 bay leaf
1 cup diced cooked chicken
$\frac{1}{2}$ cup shelled peas
4 small scallions, some green tops included, sliced
1 egg yolk
$\frac{1}{3}$ cup heavy whipping cream
4 Boston or butter lettuce leaves, shredded
salt and pepper

❇ Put the celery, carrots, and leek in a saucepan with the stock, bay leaf, and salt and pepper to taste. Cover and bring to a boil. Reduce the heat to medium, then simmer for 15 minutes, or until tender.

❇ Add the chicken, peas, and scallions. Simmer for about 8 minutes, or until the peas are just tender.

❇ Remove the pan from the heat. Lightly beat the egg yolk and cream together, and stir the mixture into the soup. Reheat gently, stirring.

❇ Ladle into warm bowls, add the lettuce, and serve immediately.

Irish Seafood Cocktail

Based on the traditional shrimp cocktail, this dish makes the most of Ireland's bountiful seafood. Crab, shrimp, and large meaty prawns are used in this recipe, but any combination will do. It's important that the seafood is particularly fresh.

Serves 4

4 crisp lettuce leaves, shredded
4-inch piece cucumber
1 cup white crabmeat
1 cup shelled, cooked shrimp
12 large, headless, cooked prawns or
    crayfish with shells
sea salt flakes
lemon slices
paprika, a few pinches

Cocktail sauce

$2/3$ cup good-quality mayonnaise
2 tablespoons ketchup
$1/2$ teaspoon Cognac
$1/4$ teaspoon Tabasco sauce

❈ To make the cocktail sauce combine all the ingredients in a pitcher, mixing well.

❈ Divide the lettuce among four cocktail glasses or ceramic bowls.

❈ Remove alternate strips of peel from the cucumber, and quarter the flesh lengthwise. Cut three of the pieces into small dice and sprinkle on top of the lettuce. Slice the remaining piece lengthwise into four sticks and set aside.

❈ Layer the crabmeat and shrimp on top of the cucumber. Season with crumbled sea salt flakes.

❈ Remove the shells from eight of the prawns. Arrange the shelled prawns on top of the crabmeat and shrimp. Season with a little more salt, then pour the sauce over the top.

❈ Garnish with the unshelled prawns, reserved cucumber sticks, and the lemon slices. Sprinkle with a pinch of paprika and serve.

Pickled Herring, Apple & Celery Salad

Herrings have always been abundant in Ireland. In this recipe, they are tossed with potatoes, crisp apples, and celery in a creamy dill-flavored dressing. If you have not eaten herring before, this is a good recipe for trying the fish for the first time.

Serves 4

8 small waxy potatoes, such as
   red-skinned new potatoes, unpeeled
6 pickled herring fillets, about
   10 ounces in total
2 red, crisp apples, unpeeled
lemon juice, for sprinkling
4 celery stalks, with leaves
2 pickles, sliced
1 romaine lettuce heart
salt and pepper

Dressing
½ cup sour cream or crème fraîche
1 tablespoon cider vinegar or white
   wine vinegar
½ teaspoon dry mustard
2 tablespoons chopped fresh dill
1 tablespoon olive oil
pinch of sugar
salt and pepper

❊ Put the unpeeled potatoes in a saucepan of salted water. Bring to a boil, then boil for about 10 minutes, or until just tender. Drain and spread out on a clean dish towel to dry. Slice thickly and set aside until cool.

❊ Meanwhile, make the dressing. Combine all the ingredients in a bowl and whisk until smooth.

❊ Cut the herring fillets into bite-size pieces. Quarter and core the apples, then slice into segments. Sprinkle the apple slices with a little lemon juice to prevent discoloration. Cut off and reserve the celery leaves, then quarter the celery stalks lengthwise and slice widthwise into 2¾-inch sticks.

❊ Put the herrings, apples, and celery in a large bowl with the sliced potatoes and pickles. Season to taste with salt and pepper and toss gently to mix.

❊ Remove the stems from the lettuce leaves, tear the leaves into large pieces, and arrange them on individual serving plates. Pile the herring mixture on top and spoon over the dressing. Garnish with the reserved celery leaves and serve immediately.

Kipper & Potato Salad with Mustard Dressing

Made with gutted and split herrings smoked over oak chips, kippers are one of Ireland's best-loved cured fish. Their tasty dense, brown flesh is excellent eaten raw in a salad, as in this recipe, but it is also good broiled or briefly boiled in water.

Serves 4–6

1½ pounds waxy new potatoes, scrubbed
3 tablespoons chopped fresh dill, plus sprigs to garnish
4 scallions, some green tops included, diagonally sliced
8 radishes, sliced
4 kipper fillets, about 2½ ounces each
salt

Mustard dressing
1 teaspoon dry mustard
pinch of sugar
salt and pepper
2 tablespoons cider vinegar
2 tablespoons heavy cream
3 tablespoons peanut oil
3 tablespoons olive oil

❈ Cook the potatoes in boiling salted water for 15–20 minutes, or until just tender. Drain and slice widthwise into ¼-inch pieces. Set aside to cool.

❈ To make the dressing, combine the mustard, sugar, salt and pepper, cider vinegar, and heavy cream. Gradually add the oils, whisking until smooth and thick.

❈ Put the potatoes in a bowl, and mix with the dressing and dill. Add most of the scallions and radishes, reserving a few to garnish. Check the seasoning, and add more salt and pepper if necessary.

❈ Remove the skin from the kipper fillets. Slice each fillet lengthwise into four, then slice each piece widthwise into thin bite-size strips.

❈ Divide the potato mixture among individual serving plates. Arrange the kipper strips attractively on top, and garnish with the reserved scallions, radishes, and dill sprigs.

Smoked Mackerel & Horseradish Pâté

Mackerel is plentiful in Ireland and is a versatile fish, used either fresh, cured, or smoked. In this recipe, it is combined with horseradish in a tasty pâté. Fresh horseradish is in season from summer to early fall in Ireland, but in the United States it is available in fall or early spring. It is also available already grated in jars.

Serves 4

8 ounces smoked mackerel fillets
finely grated zest and juice of 1 lemon
1/2 cup cream cheese
1/4 cup freshly grated horseradish or
   good-quality horseradish sauce
2 tablespoons chopped fresh parsley
1/2 teaspoon black pepper
1/2 teaspoon sea salt flakes
whole wheat toast, to serve

❈ Remove the skin and any bones from the mackerel fillets and flake the flesh.

❈ Mix the fish with the lemon zest and juice, the cream cheese, and horseradish. Mash to a spreadable consistency, then add the parsley, pepper, and sea salt. Chill until ready to serve.

❈ Serve with hot whole wheat toast.

GLENOE VILLAGE, COUNTY ANTRIM

Irish Rarebit

Meaning "tasty morsel," "rarebit" (or "rabbit") is a popular light course throughout Ireland and the British Isles, where it is traditionally served at "high tea." Numerous recipes exist, but most include cheese and mustard. Rarebit is delicious on toasted Irish soda bread, topped with chopped pickles.

Serves 4

2 cups shredded mild cheddar cheese
2 tablespoons lightly salted butter
¼ cup whole milk
1 teaspoon cider vinegar
1 teaspoon dry mustard
4 slices whole wheat or soda bread
2 tablespoons chopped dill pickles
salt and pepper

❖ Preheat the broiler until hot. Put the cheese, butter, and milk in a saucepan and heat gently, stirring, until creamy and smooth. Add the vinegar, mustard, and seasoning to the sauce.

❖ Toast the bread on only one side. Place on a baking sheet, uncooked side facing upward. Pour the sauce over the bread. Place under the preheated broiler for 2–3 minutes, until golden and bubbling.

❖ Sprinkle with the chopped pickles and serve immediately.

Bacon, Beet & Spinach Salad with Cashel Blue Cheese

Cashel Blue cheese is made near the Rock of Cashel in County Tipperary. When mature, it develops a mellow, slightly spicy flavor that goes well with beets. A good alternative would be a traditional farmhouse hard blue cheese such as Maytag Blue.

Serves 4–6

10–12 small beets, no more than
  2 inches in diameter
6 bacon strips
4 cups baby spinach
6 ounces Cashel Blue cheese, broken
  into small chunks
⅓ cup toasted hazelnuts
2 tablespoons chopped chives

Dressing
1 shallot, finely chopped
2 teaspoons white wine vinegar
1 teaspoon Dijon mustard
salt and pepper
⅓ cup extra virgin olive oil

❧ Preheat the broiler to high. Trim all but ½ inch of stem from the beets and any long roots. Leave the peel in place. Plunge into a large saucepan of boiling water, bring back to a boil, then simmer briskly for about 30 minutes, or until the beets are just tender. Drain and let cool a little.

❧ Meanwhile, broil the bacon for 4–5 minutes, turning once, until crisp. Blot with paper towels and slice widthwise into bite-size pieces. Set aside and keep warm.

❧ Whisk together the dressing ingredients in a pitcher and set aside.

❧ When the beets are cool enough to handle, remove the peel, leaving the stem in place and being careful to avoid damaging the flesh. Using a sharp knife, slice the beets in half lengthwise.

❧ Arrange the spinach leaves on a serving platter or individual plates. Whisk the dressing again and spoon a little over the leaves. Arrange the beets attractively on top and pour the remaining dressing over them. Scatter with the cheese, bacon, and nuts, finishing with a sprinkling of chives.

Chapter 2
ENTRÉES

Sea Trout with Cider & Cream Sauce

With its extensive coastline and rivers, Ireland boasts an abundance of sea trout and salmon. Here, a whole fish is cooked in foil with typically Irish flavorings—cider and leeks—which add depth of flavor to the cream sauce. The dish makes a splendid centerpiece for a special occasion.

Serves 8–10

7³/₄-pound whole sea trout or salmon, gutted
oil, for brushing
small bunch parsley, plus a few extra sprigs to garnish
2 fresh bay leaves
sea salt flakes
black pepper
1 leek, halved lengthwise and sliced
2 lemons, thinly sliced
3¹/₂ tablespoons lightly salted butter
1 cup dry hard cider
1 cup light cream
3 tablespoons chopped fresh tarragon or dill
boiled new potatoes and peas, to serve

❧ Preheat the oven to 350°F. Line a roasting pan with thick aluminum foil large enough to loosely enclose the fish in a sealed package. Brush the inside of the foil with oil.

❧ Remove the head, tail, and fins from the fish. Place the fish on the foil and stuff the cavity with the parsley and bay leaves. Rub all over with sea salt flakes and black pepper. Arrange the leek slices and half of the lemon slices over the fish, and dot with the butter. Gather up the foil and pour the cider around the fish. Seal the foil well, leaving a small vent at the top.

❧ Place the fish package in the roasting pan in the preheated oven and bake for 1¹/₄ hours, or until the thickest part of the flesh looks opaque when pierced with the tip of a knife. Open the foil and carefully slide the fish onto a warm serving platter, discarding the parsley, bay leaves, lemon, and leek. Keep warm.

❧ Transfer the juices from the foil into the pan, along with any that flow from the fish, and place on the stove over medium-high heat. Stir in the cream and tarragon, then simmer briskly for 10–15 minutes, until slightly thickened. Check the seasoning and pour into a pitcher.

❧ Remove the skin from the top of the fish. Garnish with the remaining lemon slices and parsley sprigs. Serve with the sauce, new potatoes, and peas.

Cockle & Mussel Gratin

Cockles and mussels have always been popular in Irish coastal communities. They could be collected from the shore instead of risking the potential peril of a boat. In this recipe, the two are cooked in a rich and tasty gratin. The crisp topping provides contrasting texture and flavor to the seafood below. If you can't find cockles, use small clams instead.

Serves 3–4

1³/₄ pounds mussels
¹/₂ cup water
¹/₂ cup (1 stick) lightly salted butter
2 onions, chopped
1¹/₄ cups cooked shelled cockles
juice and finely grated zest of ¹/₂ lemon
3 tablespoons chopped fresh parsley
salt and pepper
1 cup coarse bread crumbs from
  a day-old ciabatta loaf
2 garlic cloves, finely chopped

❈ Preheat the oven to 425°F. Scrub and beard the mussels, discarding any with broken shells or that remain open. Put in a large saucepan with the water. Cover and steam for 4–5 minutes, until the shells open. Discard any that remain closed. Reserve eight mussels in their shells as a garnish. Remove the rest from the shells.

❈ Melt half of the butter in a skillet over medium-high heat. Add the onions and sauté for 7 minutes, until soft but not colored. Transfer to a 2-quart gratin dish.

❈ Add the cockles, shelled mussels, lemon juice, and 2 tablespoons of the parsley. Season with salt and pepper and stir to mix.

❈ Set aside a pat of butter and melt the remaining butter. Mix with the bread crumbs, garlic, lemon zest, and remaining parsley. Season with a little more salt and pepper.

❈ Spread the bread-crumb mixture over the seafood. Top with the reserved mussels and dot them with the remaining butter.

❈ Bake in the oven for 10–15 minutes, until the crumbs are golden and crisp and the seafood is thoroughly heated. Serve immediately.

Dublin Lawyer

A luxurious dish for two, Dublin Lawyer is reputedly named after the city's wealthy lawyers and their liking for large amounts of whiskey. The dish is usually made with lobster, which is plentiful in Ireland. This version with crab is just as delicious.

Serves 2

2 large cooked crabs
2 tablespoons lightly salted butter
1 shallot, finely chopped
1/4 cup Irish whiskey
1/2 cup heavy cream
sea salt flakes
black pepper
pinch of cayenne pepper
pinch of paprika, to garnish (optional)

To serve
steamed baby carrots
steamed sea asparagus or peas

- Pull the claws and legs from the crabs and separate at the joints into sections. Crack with a mallet. Use a skewer or teaspoon to pick out the meat from all the sections except the claws. Set these aside. Pick out the meat from the body section, discarding the pointed gills (dead men's fingers), the stomach sac, and any sludgy brown sediment.

- Melt the butter in a skillet over medium heat. Add the shallot and cook for 5 minutes, until soft. Add the crabmeat and the reserved cracked claws.

- Pour in the whiskey and ignite it. When the flames die down, stir in the cream. Season with sea salt, black pepper, and a pinch of cayenne. Stir for a few minutes until heated through.

- Divide between two warm plates. Garnish with a pinch of paprika, if using. Serve with lightly cooked baby carrots and sea asparagus or peas. Use your fingers to extract the crabmeat from the claws.

Dublin Coddle

This nourishing and economical dish of bacon, sausage, and potatoes has been a favorite in Ireland, particularly in Dublin, since the seventeenth century. It is invariably served with soda bread to mop up the juices, which, if the dish has been properly "coddled," or slow-cooked, should be thick.

Serves 4–6

1 pound bacon strips
8 good-quality pork sausages
4 onions, sliced
black pepper
1 leek, some green tops included, sliced
2 bay leaves
2 sprigs thyme
1/4 cup chopped fresh parsley
2 garlic cloves, chopped
6 starchy potatoes, such as russets, peeled and cut into 2 or 3 large chunks
3 cups ham stock or chicken stock
soda bread, to serve

❇ Preheat the broiler to high and preheat the oven to 300°F. Broil the bacon for 7–8 minutes, until just starting to crisp. Drain on paper towels, slice in half widthwise, and set aside. Reserve the fat in the broiler pan.

❇ Heat a skillet over medium heat, add the sausages, and cook, turning, for about 15 minutes, until evenly browned. If necessary, use a little bacon fat to prevent the sausages from sticking. Remove the sausages from the skillet, slice in half widthwise, and set aside.

❇ Using the sausage skillet, gently cook the onions for 7 minutes, until soft but not colored. Add more bacon fat if necessary.

❇ Layer the onions, sausages, and bacon in the bottom of a flameproof casserole dish, seasoning each layer with plenty of black pepper. Add the leek, herbs, and garlic, and finish with a layer of potatoes. Season with a little more black pepper, then pour in the stock.

❇ Cover the casserole dish tightly and bring to a boil on top of the stove. Transfer to the preheated oven and cook for 45 minutes, or until the potatoes are tender.

❇ Serve with chunks of soda bread to mop up the juices.

Pork Tenderloin with Roasted Rhubarb

The pig has always been important in Ireland, and pork, either fresh or cured, features strongly in the cuisine. In this recipe, young pink rhubarb tempers the meat's natural sweetness and produces deliciously tangy juices. Use a blade-end or center-cut joint for moistness and flavor.

Serves 4

1³/₄-pound boneless pork tenderloin
olive oil
1 teaspoon sea salt flakes
¹/₂ teaspoon black pepper
10 small sprigs of rosemary
¹/₂ cup chicken stock
3¹/₂ pink rhubarb stalks, trimmed and
    diagonally sliced into 1¹/₂-inch lengths
1 tablespoon honey

❈ Preheat the oven to 375°F. Using the tip of a sharp knife, score the fat, but not the flesh, of the pork at ¹/₂-inch intervals. Tie the meat with kitchen twine to form a neat roll. You can ask your butcher to do both of these.

❈ Place the meat in a small roasting pan. Rub with oil, and then with the sea salt and black pepper, rubbing them in well. Insert the rosemary sprigs into the slits in the fat. Roast in the preheated oven for 40 minutes.

❈ Pour in the stock. Arrange the rhubarb around the meat and drizzle with the honey. Roast for another 10–15 minutes, until the rhubarb is tender and starting to color at the edges.

❈ Transfer the pork and rhubarb to a warm serving platter, reserving the pan juices. Make a tent over the meat with aluminum foil, and let rest for 10 minutes in a warm place.

❈ Place the roasting pan on the stove over medium-high heat. Let bubble rapidly to reduce the pan juices, including any that have flowed from the meat, for 3–4 minutes, until slightly thickened. Check the seasoning, strain into a pitcher, and serve with the meat.

Ham with Parsley Sauce

This is a comforting dish still worthy of serving at dinnertime. Make sure the steaks are "green" (the term used for unsmoked fresh ham), because smoked ham is too salty. Cut the steaks thick, otherwise the meat will dry out during cooking. Buy a small, boneless ham joint and slice it into steaks yourself.

Serves 4

1¾-pound fresh ham, cut into four
  ¾-inch-thick steaks
vegetable oil, for brushing

Parsley sauce
2 tablespoons unsalted butter
1 shallot, finely chopped
3 tablespoons all-purpose flour
¾ cup ham or chicken stock
1 cup whole milk
⅓ cup chopped fresh parsley
squeeze of lemon juice
½ teaspoon dry mustard
salt and white pepper

❖ First make the parsley sauce. Melt the butter in a skillet over medium–low heat. Add the shallot and cook for 2–3 minutes, until soft but not colored.

❖ Remove the skillet from the heat and stir in the flour. Return to the heat and cook for 1 minute, stirring. Reduce the heat to low, and whisk in the stock and milk. Keep whisking until the sauce starts to bubble. Stir in the parsley, then add the lemon juice, mustard, pepper, and a pinch of salt. Simmer gently, stirring often, for 20 minutes.

❖ Meanwhile, remove the rind, but not the fat, from the ham steaks. Slash the fat at ¾-inch intervals. Brush with oil on both sides.

❖ Heat a ridged grill pan over high heat. Cook the steaks on one side for 5–6 minutes. Once they start to color on the underside, cover with a lid and reduce the heat to medium. Turn and cook the other side for 5 minutes, covered.

❖ Place the steaks on warm serving plates, pour the sauce over them, and serve.

Blood Sausage with Caramelized Pear and Cider

Made from boiled pig's blood bound with barley or other grain, the blood sausage, called "black pudding" in Ireland, is a heavy-duty sausage that evolved from the need to use every part of the pig. It is popular at breakfast time in Ireland, where it is currently undergoing something of a renaissance, and modern chefs are using it in a variety of novel ways.

Serves 4

3¹/₂ tablespoons lightly salted butter
3 firm pears, such as Bosc, peeled, cored, and quartered lengthwise
12 ounces blood sausage, thickly sliced
2 shallots, chopped
¹/₂ cup chicken stock
¹/₂ cup dry hard cider
sea salt flakes
black pepper
¹/₂ cup light cream
squeeze of lemon juice
3 tablespoons chopped fresh parsley

❖ Heat half of the butter in a heavy skillet. When it sizzles, sauté the pear segments over medium-low heat for 10 minutes, turning, until caramelized at the edges. Remove from the skillet and keep warm.

❖ Add the blood sausage slices to the skillet and cook for 3 minutes on each side side, turning them carefully so that they don't disintegrate. Set aside and keep warm.

❖ Pour off the fat and wipe the skillet clean with paper towels. Heat the remaining butter in the skillet, add the shallots, and cook for 3–4 minutes, until softened.

❖ Pour in the stock and cider, raise the heat, and bring to a boil. Reduce the heat a little, then simmer briskly for 5–7 minutes, until reduced by half. Season with sea salt and plenty of pepper.

❖ Add the cream to the skillet and simmer for about a minute, until slightly thickened.

❖ Return the pear slices to the skillet, add a squeeze of lemon, and cook for an additional minute, or until heated through. Sprinkle with the parsley and serve with the sausage slices.

Beef & Stout Pies

The Irish love their main-course pies—hot, warm, or cold, eaten at home, in a restaurant, or outdoors. These individual puff-pastry pies are made with richly flavored meat stock and stout, usually Guinness, which the Irish claim is the only dark ale suitable for cooking beef.

Serves 4

3 tablespoons all-purpose flour
1 teaspoon salt
1/2 teaspoon black pepper
2 pounds boneless chuck steak
  or eye of round steak, cut into
  1-inch pieces
vegetable oil, for frying
1 1/4 cups meat stock
1 onion, coarsely chopped
8 ounces cremini mushrooms,
  stems discarded, caps quartered
1 tablespoon tomato paste
2 teaspoons chopped fresh thyme
1 cup stout
1 pound store-bought puff pastry
1 egg yolk, lightly beaten

❧ Combine the flour, salt, and pepper in a bowl, then toss the beef in the mixture until evenly coated.

❧ Heat 3 tablespoons of oil in a large skillet over medium-high heat. Cook the beef, in batches, and transfer to a flameproof casserole dish. Deglaze the skillet with 1/4 cup of stock, and add the liquid to the casserole dish.

❧ Heat another 1–2 tablespoons of oil in the skillet and cook the onion and mushrooms for 6–7 minutes, until soft. Add to the casserole dish with the tomato paste, thyme, stout, and remaining stock. Heat the casserole dish over medium-high heat, bring to a boil, then simmer gently with the lid slightly askew for 1 1/2 hours. Check the seasoning.

❧ Drain the meat mixture in a strainer set over a bowl, reserving the liquid. Let rest until cool.

❧ Preheat the oven to 425°F. Put a baking sheet in the oven to heat.

❧ Divide the meat mixture among four individual 1 3/4-cup pie plates with a flat rim or ovenproof bowls. Pour in enough of the liquid to not quite cover the filling. Dampen the rims of the pie plates.

❧ Cut the pastry into quarters. Roll out each piece to about 1 inch bigger than the pie plates. From each quarter, cut a 1/2-inch strip and press it onto a dampened rim. Brush with egg yolk, then drape the pastry quarter on top, covering the strip. Trim, crimp the edges with a fork, and make three slashes down the middle. Decorate the tops with shapes cut from the trimmings. Brush with the remaining egg yolk.

❧ Place the pies on the preheated baking sheet and bake in the preheated oven for 20 minutes. Reduce the heat to 400°F and bake for an additional 5 minutes.

Slow-Roasted Shoulder of Lamb with Herb Dumplings

Like many traditional Irish lamb dishes, this is nourishing and delicious and made with an economical cut. The meat is slow-roasted at low heat until almost falling off the bone. Light and fluffy herb-flavored dumplings mop up the flavorsome juices.

Serves 4–6

2 large carrots, cut into thin sticks
1 onion, sliced
3¹/₄-pound bone-in shoulder of lamb
2–3 fresh bay leaves
1 sage sprig
small bunch parsley
salt and pepper
2¹/₂ cups meat stock

Herb-flavored dumplings
1 cup all-purpose flour
1 teaspoon baking powder
¹/₂ teaspoon salt
¹/₄ teaspoon black pepper
1¹/₂ tablespoons finely chopped fresh parsley
1¹/₂ tablespoons finely chopped fresh mint or herb of your choice
2 tablespoons lightly salted butter
1 egg
2 tablespoons milk

❋ Preheat the oven to 450°F. Scatter the carrots and onion over the bottom of a roasting pan slightly larger than the meat. Place the meat on top, tucking the herbs underneath. Season with salt and pepper, then pour in enough stock to not quite cover the vegetables.

❋ Cover the pan with thick aluminum foil, sealing the edges well. Roast in the preheated oven for 20 minutes, then reduce the heat to 325°F and roast for an additional 3 hours.

❋ To make the dumplings, sift the flour, baking powder, and salt into a bowl. Mix in the black pepper and herbs. Rub in the butter until the mixture resembles coarse bread crumbs. Beat together the egg and milk in a pitcher, then stir into the flour mixture to make a soft, slightly sticky dough.

❋ With floured hands, divide the dough into 12 pieces and roll into balls. Drop into a large saucepan of boiling salted water. Partially cover and cook for 15 minutes. Using tongs, gently lift the dumplings into a colander and let drain for a few minutes. Transfer to a plate until needed.

❋ Just before the meat is ready, heat the remaining stock in a small saucepan. Remove the meat from the oven and open up the foil. Arrange the dumplings around the meat and pour in the hot stock. Reseal the foil and roast for another 15 minutes.

❋ Transfer the meat to a warm platter and discard the herbs. Arrange the dumplings and vegetables around the meat. Strain the juices into a pitcher and serve with the meat.

Roast Goose with Apple Stuffing & Cider Gravy

In days gone by, it was customary in Ireland to eat a young goose on Michaelmas Day (September 29). According to Irish folklore, doing so provided protection from financial hardship. Michaelmas also coincided with the apple harvest, hence the tradition of an apple-based stuffing, as in this recipe, and applesauce as an accompaniment.

Serves 4–5

1 x 8³/₄-pound goose, with the giblets (the neck, heart, and gizzard) and lumps of fat in the cavity reserved, and wing tips and leg tips cut off and reserved
1 onion, coarsely chopped
1 celery stalk, coarsely chopped
1 large carrot, coarsely chopped
handful of parsley
2–3 thyme sprigs
2 fresh bay leaves
¹/₂ teaspoon black peppercorns
2 small firm apples
1 cup hard dry cider
2 tablespoons apple cider vinegar
2 tablespoons all-purpose flour
salt and pepper

Apple stuffing

3 onions, chopped
4 unsmoked bacon strips, chopped
4 starchy potatoes, such as russets, peeled and cut into ¹/₂-inch dice
3 cooking apples, such as Granny Smith or Gravenstein, quartered, cored, peeled, and coarsely chopped
1¹/₂ tablespoons chopped fresh sage
1 tablespoon chopped fresh thyme
¹/₂ teaspoon sea salt
¹/₄ teaspoon black pepper
4 ounces goose liver, chopped
2 tablespoons chopped fresh parsley
finely grated zest of 1 lemon

❖ Prick the goose all over with a fork and place in a colander. Douse with plenty of boiling water, then pat dry with paper towels. Season inside the cavity with salt and pepper, and rub salt all over the skin. Let dry.

❖ To make the stuffing, heat a pat of goose fat in a skillet over medium heat, add the onion, and cook until soft. Add the bacon, potatoes, apples, sage, thyme, salt, and pepper. Gently cook, covered, for 20 minutes, until the apples are soft. Add the liver, parsley, and lemon zest, and cook for 5 minutes. Spread out the stuffing in a wide bowl and let cool.

❖ Meanwhile, make a stock. Put the reserved wing and leg tips and giblets in a saucepan. Add the vegetables, herbs, and peppercorns. Pour in enough cold water to just cover. Slowly bring to a boil, covered, reduce the heat, and simmer with the lid askew for 2 hours.

❖ Preheat the oven to 400°F. Spoon the stuffing into the goose cavity. Insert a small apple at each end to hold the stuffing in place, then seal the flaps with toothpicks. Truss the wings and legs with twine. Put the goose in a roasting pan and cook for 30 minutes, then pour off the fat. Reduce the temperature to 350°F. Cover the goose loosely with aluminum foil and cook for 1¹/₂ hours, pouring off the fat twice again at 30-minute intervals. Add a little water if the pan looks dry. Remove the foil and roast for 30 minutes, until the juices run clear when the thickest part of the thigh is pierced with a sharp knife. Lift the goose onto a warm platter, cover with foil, and let rest for 20 minutes.

❖ To make the gravy, strain 2 cups of stock and blot up any fat that rises. Pour off the fat from the roasting pan. Stir in the cider and vinegar, heat over medium heat, scraping up any sediment in the pan. Add the flour and stir for a minute, until blended. Pour in the strained stock. Bring to a boil, simmer for 5 minutes, and strain.

❖ Slice the apples and arrange around the goose. Carve the goose and serve with the sliced apples, stuffing, and cider gravy.

Chapter 3

VEGETABLES & SIDES

Roasted Beet Packages with Horseradish Butter

Fresh beets are gaining popularity among Irish chefs. In this recipe, the beets are roasted in a foil package, producing wonderfully concentrated flavors and fragrant juices. Horseradish butter makes a piquant contrast to the sweetness of the beets.

Serves 4

8 small beets, peeled and halved
  lengthwise
olive oil
4 thyme sprigs
sea salt flakes
black pepper

Horseradish butter
$^1/_2$ cup (1 stick) unsalted butter,
  at room temperature
$^1/_4$ cup fresh grated horseradish
$^1/_2$ teaspoon sea salt flakes
$^1/_2$ teaspoon black pepper

❋ Preheat the oven to 375°F. Put the beets in a bowl and toss with enough olive oil to coat.

❋ Place four beet halves and a thyme sprig on a thick square of aluminum foil. Season with sea salt flakes and black pepper. Wrap in a loose package, sealing the edges well. Repeat with the remaining beets.

❋ Cook the beets in the preheated oven for about 1 hour, or until you can pierce the beets with a toothpick.

❋ Meanwhile, make the horseradish butter. Mash all the ingredients with a fork, mixing well. Scrape the mixture onto a piece of plastic wrap and form into a log. Chill in the refrigerator.

❋ When the beets are tender, open the foil and add a slice of horseradish butter. Serve immediately, still in the packages.

Sticky Carrots with Whiskey & Ginger Glaze

Comforting carrots take on a new lease of life sizzled in butter with snippets of ginger. The juices reduce to a delicious syrupy glaze, while a glug of whiskey gives the dish an Irish touch.

Serves 2–3

1 teaspoon sugar
$^1/_2$ teaspoon black pepper
good pinch of sea salt flakes
$^1/_4$ cup peanut oil
3 tablespoons lightly salted butter
4 large carrots (about 1 pound), diagonally sliced into $^1/_2$-inch circles
$^3/_4$-inch piece fresh ginger, sliced into matchstick strips
2 tablespoons Irish whiskey
$^1/_2$ cup chicken stock or vegetable stock

❧ Combine the sugar, pepper, and sea salt and set aside.

❧ Heat the oil and half of the butter in a large skillet. Add the carrots in a single layer and sprinkle with the sugar mixture. Cook over medium-high heat for 3 minutes, then start turning the slices with tongs and reduce the heat if necessary. When slightly browned on both sides and starting to blacken at the edges, transfer the carrots to a plate.

❧ Clean the skillet with paper towels. Add the ginger and cook over medium-high heat for 1–2 minutes, until golden. Add to the carrots.

❧ Add the remaining butter, the whiskey, and stock. Bring to a boil, then simmer for 3 minutes or until syrupy. Return the carrots and ginger to the skillet, and swirl with the syrup for 1 minute. Serve immediately.

Champ

One of Ireland's most delicious side dishes, champ is made with creamy mashed potatoes mixed with chives or scallions, piled high in a bowl with a pool of melted butter in the center. It was traditionally served at Halloween, when it was customary to leave a bowl under a bush for the fairies.

Serves 4

8 starchy potatoes (about 2 pounds), such as russets or Yukon gold, peeled and cut into even chunks

20 scallions, some green tops included, chopped

1¹/₂ cups milk

¹/₄ teaspoon white peppercorns

¹/₄ cup snipped chives

1 teaspoon sea salt flakes

¹/₂ cup (1 stick) lightly salted butter, melted and hot

❖ Add the potatoes to a large saucepan of salted boiling water, cover, bring back to a boil, and simmer gently for 20 minutes, until tender. Drain well and put back in the pan. Cover with a clean dish towel for a few minutes to get rid of excess moisture.

❖ While the potatoes are cooking, put the chopped scallions in a saucepan with the milk and peppercorns. Simmer for 5 minutes, then drain, reserving the milk and scallions separately.

❖ Mash the potatoes until smooth, stirring in enough of the reserved milk to produce a creamy consistency. Stir in the scallions and chives. Season to taste with sea salt flakes and more pepper if necessary.

❖ Transfer the potato mixture to a warm serving dish. Make a well in the center and pour in the hot, melted butter. Serve immediately, mixing in the melted butter at the table.

Roasted Leeks with Parsley

An all-time Irish favorite, leeks are given a Mediterranean treatment in this quickly prepared dish. Roasted until slightly charred, the leeks make a tasty accompaniment to either fish or roast lamb.

Serves 4

4 large leeks, trimmed and halved
  lengthwise
3 tablespoons extra virgin olive oil
sea salt flakes
black pepper
1 tablespoon chopped fresh
  flat-leaf parsley

❈ Preheat the oven to 475°F. Pack the leeks in a single layer in a shallow casserole dish into which they fit tightly.

❈ Brush with the olive oil, making sure it goes into the crevices. Sprinkle with the sea salt flakes, black pepper, and parsley, turning to coat.

❈ Roast in the preheated oven for 15–20 minutes, turning once, until the leeks begin to blacken at the edges.

BUNRATTY FOLK PARK, COUNTY CLARE

Roasted Banana Shallots with Bread Crumbs & Cheddar

A stalwart of Irish cuisine, onions take pride of place in this tasty gratin. Topped with crisp bread crumbs and Irish cheddar cheese, the dish is equally suitable as a vegetarian main course or an accompaniment to roast beef or lamb.

Serves 4–6

8 banana shallots or small-to-
  medium onions
2 tablespoons apple juice concentrate
6 tablespoons olive oil or canola oil
$\frac{1}{2}$ tablespoon finely chopped fresh
  thyme or rosemary
$\frac{1}{4}$ teaspoon black pepper
sea salt flakes
$\frac{2}{3}$ cup coarse stale bread crumbs
1 cup shredded mild Irish
  cheddar cheese
1 tablespoon chopped fresh parsley,
  to garnish

❦ Preheat the oven to 425°F. Peel the banana shallots, slice in half lengthwise, and put in a shallow bowl.

❦ Whisk together the apple juice concentrate, 4 tablespoons of the olive oil, and the thyme. Pour the mixture over the shallots, turning to coat well.

❦ Transfer the contents of the bowl into a small nonstick roasting pan in which the shallots fit in a single layer. Turn the shallots cut-side up and season with the pepper and a good pinch of sea salt flakes. Sprinkle with the bread crumbs and the remaining oil.

❦ Roast in the preheated oven for 25–30 minutes, or until the shallots are soft and the edges are beginning to blacken. Scatter the shredded cheese over the top, and roast for an additional 3 minutes, or until the cheese is melted and bubbling.

❦ Garnish with the parsley and serve immediately.

Buttered Kale with Chives & Lemon

Kale is a sturdy crop that features regularly on the Irish menu, particularly in winter. In this recipe, it is lightly cooked and seasoned with lemon zest and chives to complement the rich and earthy flavor.

Serves 4–6

8 ounces kale
grated zest of 1 lemon
$1/3$ cup snipped chives
large pat of lightly salted butter
sea salt flakes
white pepper

- Remove the tough stems from the kale, then stack the leaves and slice into wide ribbons. Place in a steamer basket set over boiling water. Steam for 10–12 minutes, until tender but still bright green.

- Transfer the kale to a warm serving dish, add the lemon zest, chives, and butter, and toss together. Season with sea salt flakes and pepper. Serve immediately.

BOTANIC GARDENS, BELFAST

Red Cabbage with Mushrooms, Nuts & Bacon

A major feature of Irish cuisine, cabbage comes in a cornucopia of appetizing colors and flavors. In this recipe, red cabbage is lightly braised with bacon, mushrooms, and crunchy nuts and is a superb accompaniment to roast goose or pork.

Serves 4

½ large red cabbage
2 tablespoons canola oil or vegetable oil
6 thin bacon strips, cut into
   bite-size pieces
1 onion, chopped
2 teaspoons thyme leaves
2½ cups coarsely chopped cremini
   mushrooms
⅓ cup toasted hazelnuts,
   coarsely chopped
grated zest of 1 lemon
1 teaspoon sea salt flakes
½ teaspoon black pepper
½ teaspoon sugar
2 tablespoons apple cider vinegar
1 cup meat stock
¼ cup chopped fresh parsley
pat of lightly salted butter

� Quarter the cabbage lengthwise and discard the tough core in the center. Slice the leaves widthwise into ribbons.

✷ Heat the oil in a flameproof casserole dish or deep skillet over medium-high heat. Cook the bacon for about 5 minutes, until crisp.

✷ Reduce the heat to medium, add the onion and thyme, and cook for 5 minutes, until the onion is translucent.

✷ Add the mushrooms and cabbage, and cook for an additional 5 minutes, until starting to soften.

✷ Stir in the nuts, lemon zest, sea salt, pepper, and sugar, and cook for an additional 3 minutes. Pour in the vinegar and stock, cover, and bring to a boil, then reduce the heat and simmer for 15 minutes, until the cabbage is tender.

✷ Check the seasoning, adding salt and pepper if necessary. Stir in the parsley and a pat of butter just before serving.

Bacon & Potato Cakes

Mashed potatoes have been a staple in the Irish kitchen for centuries. In this recipe, they are mixed with bacon snippets and oats, another staple, then fried in cakes until crisp. A topping of watercress sprigs and a strip of crisp bacon gives the cakes a stylish touch.

Serves 4

5 starchy potatoes, such as russets or Yukon gold, peeled and cut into even chunks

8 thin bacon strips

1 tablespoon lightly salted butter

1/2 teaspoon sea salt flakes

1/2 teaspoon black pepper

2 tablespoons snipped chives

1/4 cup rolled oats

1 egg, lightly beaten

all-purpose flour, for dusting

canola oil or vegetable oil, for frying

watercress sprigs, to garnish

- Add the potatoes to a large saucepan of salted boiling water, cover, bring back to a boil, and simmer gently for 20 minutes, until tender. Drain well and put back in the pan. Cover with a clean dish towel for a few minutes to get rid of excess moisture.

- While the potatoes are cooking, cook the bacon over medium-high heat for 5–6 minutes, until crisp. Drain on paper towels. Set aside 4 strips and keep warm. Chop the remaining strips finely.

- Mash the potatoes with the butter, sea salt, and pepper until creamy. Stir in the chopped bacon, chives, oats, and beaten egg.

- With floured hands, form the potato mixture into four flat cakes about 2¾ inches in diameter.

- Heat about ½ inch of oil in a heavy saucepan over medium heat. Add the potato cakes and cook for about 4 minutes on each side, until golden brown.

- Transfer the potato cakes to warm serving plates. Top with the watercress and reserved bacon strips, and serve immediately.

Boxty Bread

The Irish have always been adept at baking, making do with the simplest of ingredients and equipment. This traditional bread is made with potato and wheat flour dough, shaped into flat circles. It makes a delicious afternoon snack served warm with plenty of butter or cheese and pickles.

Makes 4 small loaves

7 starchy potatoes (about 1³/₄ pounds), such as russets or Yukon gold
2 tablespoons lightly salted butter, plus extra to serve
²/₃ cup milk
2 teaspoons salt
¹/₂ teaspoon black pepper
1¹/₂ teaspoons dill seeds or caraway seeds (optional)
2³/₄ cups all-purpose flour, plus extra for dusting
5 teaspoons baking powder

❖ Preheat the oven to 375°F. Peel four of the potatoes, cut them into even chunks, and bring to a boil in a large saucepan of salted water. Cover and simmer gently for about 20 minutes, until tender. Drain well and put back in the pan. Cover with a clean dish towel for a few minutes to get rid of excess moisture. Mash with the butter until smooth.

❖ Meanwhile, peel the remaining three potatoes and grate coarsely. Wrap in a clean piece of cheesecloth and squeeze tightly to remove the moisture. Put the grated potatoes in a large bowl with the milk, ³/₄ teaspoon of the salt, the pepper, and dill seeds, if using. Beat in the mashed potatoes.

❖ Sift the flour, baking powder, and remaining salt onto the potato mixture. Mix to a smooth dough, adding a little more flour if the mixture is too soft.

❖ Knead lightly, then shape into four flat, round loaves about 4 inches in diameter. Place on a nonstick baking sheet. Mark each loaf with a large cross. Bake in the preheated oven for 40 minutes, or until well-risen and golden brown.

❖ Break each loaf into quarters. Serve warm, spread with butter.

Brown Soda Bread with Molasses

In rural Ireland bread was always made at home. It was baked on the griddle or in a cooking pot, and was usually dense-textured as yeast was rarely used as the raising agent. The introduction of baking soda in the nineteenth century made it possible for families to produce quickly made risen bread for which Ireland is now famous.

Makes 1 loaf

2 cups all-purpose flour,
    plus extra for dusting
2 cups whole wheat flour
1/2 cup rolled oats
1 1/2 teaspoons salt
1 teaspoon baking soda
1 3/4 cups buttermilk
2 tablespoons molasses

❈ Preheat the oven to 450°F. Line a baking sheet with a sheet of nonstick parchment paper.

❈ Combine the flours, oats, salt, and baking soda in a large bowl, mixing thoroughly.

❈ Whisk together the buttermilk and molasses in a large pitcher. Make a well in the center of the flour mixture and pour in the buttermilk mixture. Using a fork, stir the liquid, gradually drawing in the flour from around the edge. With floured hands, lightly knead to a soft dough.

❈ Shape the dough into a circle and place on the lined baking sheet. Press flat to about 2 inches thick. Use a sharp knife with a long blade to cut a deep cross on the top.

❈ Bake in the preheated oven for 15 minutes, then reduce the oven temperature to 400°F. Bake for an additional 20-25 minutes, or until the bottom of the bread sounds hollow when tapped. Transfer to a wire rack and let cool slightly. Serve warm.

Chapter 4

DESSERTS & DRINKS

Irish Whiskey Trifle

Trifle is said to have a "powerful stronghold" in Ireland, with every family having its favorite recipe that is, of course, better than anyone else's. This version contains the usual Irish whiskey and sherry, but you could use fruit juice for soaking if you prefer a nonalcoholic version.

Serves 8

10 ladyfingers or 1 stale sponge cake
raspberry jam, for spreading
2 macaroons, lightly crushed
finely grated zest of 1 lemon
2 tablespoons Irish whiskey
1/2 cup sherry
1 1/4 cups heavy cream
1/2 tablespoon sugar
1 cup raspberries
candied violets or miniature macaroons,
  to decorate

Custard

5 egg yolks, lightly beaten
1/4 cup sugar
2 teaspoons cornstarch
1/2 cup whole milk
1 cup heavy cream
1/2 teaspoon vanilla extract

❇ First make the custard. Combine the egg yolks and sugar in a mixing bowl. Stir in the cornstarch and mix to a smooth paste, then whisk in the milk.

❇ Heat the cream in a heavy saucepan until just starting to simmer but not boiling. Gradually whisk the hot cream into the egg mixture, then return the mixture to the pan. Whisk continuously over medium heat for about 5 minutes, until thickened. Immediately pour into a pitcher and stir in the vanilla extract. Cover with plastic wrap to prevent a skin from forming and let stand to cool completely.

❇ Thickly spread half of the ladyfingers with raspberry jam. Place the remaining ladyfingers on top to make a sandwich. If using sponge cake, slice horizontally into two or three layers and spread with jam. Arrange in a single layer in the bottom of a deep serving dish. Sprinkle with the crushed macaroons and the lemon zest.

❇ Combine the whiskey and sherry and pour over the ladyfinger mixture. Let soak for 1 hour.

❇ Spoon the cooled custard over the ladyfinger mixture.

❇ Whip the cream with the sugar until stiff peaks form. Spread over the custard, leveling with a spatula. Cover with plastic wrap and chill for 1 hour, or until ready to serve.

❇ Arrange the raspberries on top and decorate with candied violets or miniature macaroons.

Chocolate & Stout Ice Cream

This extremely rich, dark ice cream is perfect for a St. Patrick's Day celebration. Served cold, the stout flavor is subtle and perfectly matched by dark, bittersweet chocolate. For an extra-special touch, splash a little Irish Cream liqueur over each serving.

Makes about 3½ cups

1½ cups whole milk
¾ cup sugar
5½ ounces semisweet dark chocolate (at least 85 percent cocoa solids), broken into small pieces
4 egg yolks
1 teaspoon vanilla extract
1⅓ cups stout
1 cup heavy cream
grated chocolate, to decorate

❧ Pour the milk into a saucepan and add the sugar. Bring to a boil, stirring, until the sugar has dissolved. Remove from the heat and stir in the chocolate.

❧ Pour the egg yolks into a heatproof bowl and beat for 5 minutes, or until the beaters leave a faint trail when lifted from the mixture. Stir some of the warm chocolate mixture into the egg yolks, then gradually beat in the rest.

❧ Place the bowl over a saucepan of gently boiling water. Stir continuously for about 10 minutes, until the mixture reaches a temperature of 185°F, or is thick enough to coat the back of a spoon. Be careful not to let it boil.

❧ Strain the mixture through a fine strainer into a pitcher. Stir in the vanilla extract. Sit the bottom of the pitcher in iced water until cold, then cover with plastic wrap and chill for 2 hours.

❧ Meanwhile, pour the stout into a saucepan and bring to a boil. Reduce the heat and simmer briskly for 8 minutes, until reduced to 1 cup. Pour into a pitcher, let cool, then chill in the refrigerator.

❧ Stir the cream and chilled stout into the chocolate mixture, mixing well. Pour the mixture into the bowl of an ice cream machine. Churn and freeze following the manufacturer's instructions. Alternatively, pour the mixture into a shallow freezerproof container, cover with plastic wrap, and freeze for about 2 hours, until beginning to harden around the edges. Beat until smooth to get rid of any ice crystals. Freeze again, repeat the process twice, then freeze until completely firm.

❧ Move the ice cream to the refrigerator 30 minutes before serving to soften. Serve in chilled dishes, sprinkled with grated chocolate.

Oatmeal & Raspberry Cream

Oats became important to the Irish during the potato famine in the mid-nineteenth century. In this recipe, they are folded into an irresistible concoction of raspberries and whiskey- and honey-flavored cream. The dish was traditionally served to celebrate the end of the annual harvest. It is rich, so the portions are small.

Serves 6

1 cup rolled oats
1½ cups heavy cream
½ cup light cream
3 tablespoons Irish whiskey
2 tablespoons honey,
   plus extra for drizzling
2½ cups raspberries

❧ Preheat the broiler to medium. Spread out the oats on a baking sheet, place under the preheated broiler, and toast for 4–5 minutes, or until golden brown, stirring often to prevent burning. Transfer to a shallow bowl and let cool.

❧ Combine the two creams, whiskey, and honey in a mixing bowl. Stir in the oats, mixing well. Cover with plastic wrap and let rest in the refrigerator for at least 2 hours or overnight to thicken. Stir occasionally to break up any clumps of oats.

❧ Set aside ⅓ cup of the best raspberries to decorate. Lightly swirl the remaining raspberries into the oat mixture, creating attractive pink streaks. Spoon into glass serving dishes and decorate with the reserved raspberries. Drizzle with honey just before serving.

Irish Spiced Fruitcake

This traditional cake is a typical Irish afternoon treat. Unsweetened dried cherries give it a pleasing tang, as do ginger and allspice. The cake will keep for several days wrapped in wax paper and stored in an airtight container.

Makes one 8-inch cake

1½ cups mixed dried fruit, such as
  golden raisins, currants, and raisins
⅔ cup dried unsweetened cherries
⅓ cup coarsely chopped walnuts
¾ cup demerara sugar or other
  raw sugar
½ cup (1 stick) butter
1 teaspoon allspice
1 teaspoon ground ginger
½ teaspoon baking soda
1 cup milk
1¾ cups self-rising flour
2 eggs, lightly beaten

❧ Put all the ingredients apart from the flour and eggs into a saucepan and mix well. Bring to a boil over medium-high heat, stirring continuously. Reduce the heat slightly and simmer for 5 minutes, stirring occasionally. Remove from the heat and let cool for about 30 minutes.

❧ Meanwhile, preheat the oven to 350°F. Grease and line a deep 8-inch cake pan.

❧ Add the flour and eggs to the cake batter, mixing well to combine. Spoon the batter into the prepared pan, leveling the surface with a wet spatula.

❧ Bake in the preheated oven for 30 minutes. Reduce the oven temperature to 325°F and bake for an additional 1½ hours, or until a toothpick inserted in the center comes out clean.

❧ Let the cake cool in the pan for 10 minutes, then invert onto a wire rack and let cool completely.

Porter Cake

Porter, or stout, is a special type of dark beer first brewed in Ireland in the eighteenth century. Guinness is an extra-strong porter that provides color and flavor without being too overwhelming. Stored in an airtight container, this rich, moist fruitcake is best eaten several days after baking.

Makes one 7-inch cake

3 cups mixed currants and golden raisins
1 cup dried unsweetened cherries
3/4 cup finely chopped candied citrus peel
1 1/3 cups stout
2 3/4 cups all-purpose flour
1 teaspoon baking powder
1 teaspoon allspice
pinch of salt
1 cup (2 sticks) butter
1 cup firmly packed brown sugar
3 eggs, lightly beaten

❈ Mix the currants, golden raisins, cherries, and citrus peel in a large bowl. Add the stout and let soak for at least 5 hours or overnight, stirring occasionally.

❈ Preheat the oven to 325°F. Grease and line a 7-inch square cake pan.

❈ Sift the flour, baking powder, spice, and salt into a large bowl.

❈ Cream the butter and sugar in a separate bowl for about 4 minutes, until light and fluffy. Stir in the beaten eggs, a little at a time, adding some of the flour mixture at each addition and beating well. Stir in the remaining flour.

❈ Add the fruit and any liquid to the batter, mixing well to a soft consistency. Spoon the batter into the prepared pan, leveling the surface with a wet spatula.

❈ Bake in the preheated oven for 1 hour. Reduce the oven temperature to 300°F and bake for an additional 1 1/2–2 hours, or until a toothpick inserted in the center comes out clean. Let rest in the pan until completely cool.

❈ Invert, wrap in wax paper, and store in an airtight container.

Molasses Bread

Popular throughout Ireland, where it's called treacle bread—in this recipe, the treacle is replaced with molasses—this moist, dense quick bread is easy to make and keeps well. It is always served thickly spread with butter, and invariably comes with a strong cup of tea. It is also delicious spread with cream cheese.

Makes 1 loaf

1³/₄ cups all-purpose flour
1 teaspoon baking soda
¹/₂ teaspoon allspice
¹/₂ teaspoon ground ginger
5 tablespoons lightly salted butter, plus extra to serve
3 tablespoons molasses
2 eggs, lightly beaten
¹/₄ cup buttermilk
¹/₂ cup firmly packed brown sugar
¹/₃ cup currants
¹/₃ cup golden raisins

❖ Preheat the oven to 350°F. Grease and line a small 6¹/₂-x 3³/₄-inch loaf pan.

❖ Sift the flour, baking soda, and spices into a bowl. Lightly rub in the butter until the mixture resembles fine crumbs.

❖ Whisk the molasses with the eggs and buttermilk, then stir in the sugar. Make a well in the center of the flour mixture and pour in the molasses mixture. Mix with a fork, gradually drawing in the flour from around the edges.

❖ Add the currants and golden raisins, and mix to a soft dough. Spoon the dough into the prepared loaf pan, leveling the surface with a wet spatula.

❖ Bake in the preheated oven for 45–55 minutes, or until a toothpick inserted in the center comes out clean.

❖ Let cool in the pan for 15 minutes, then invert onto a wire rack and let rest for about 2 hours to cool completely.

❖ Serve spread thickly with butter.

Currant Shortbread

Shortbread is usually associated with Scotland, but similar versions are made throughout Ireland. As with many Irish dishes, each region, and often each family, has its own treasured recipe. This one includes currants and lemon zest for flavor, and ground rice for crunch.

Makes 12 wedges

1$\frac{1}{3}$ cups all-purpose flour
pinch of salt
$\frac{1}{2}$ cup ground rice or fine semolina
$\frac{3}{4}$ cup (1$\frac{1}{2}$ sticks) lightly salted butter, softened
$\frac{1}{3}$ cup superfine sugar, plus extra for dredging
finely grated zest of 1 lemon
$\frac{1}{4}$ cup dried currants

❧ Preheat the oven to 325°F. Sift the flour and salt into a bowl, and mix in the ground rice.

❧ Beat together the butter, sugar, and lemon zest in a separate bowl. Stir in the flour mixture and currants. Work the dough with your hands until it clumps together. Mold into a flattened ball and place on a nonstick baking sheet.

❧ Use your fingers to press the dough into a 9$\frac{1}{2}$-inch circle (use a small dinner plate as a guide). Lightly level the surface with a rolling pin and trim the edges neatly. Make indentations around the edge with the back of a fork, and prick the surface all over to stop it from puffing up. Mark the top into 12 equal segments with a knife.

❧ Bake in the preheated oven for 30–35 minutes, or until pale golden all over.

❧ Remove from the oven and dredge with sugar. Cut through the marked segments, then let cool and firm up.

Custard Tarts

Custard tarts are a familiar sight in Irish bakeries. This version, made with crisp, light puff pastry and a cinnamon-scented filling, is similar to the Portuguese custard tarts that are increasingly popular among modern chefs. The tarts are best eaten on the day they're made, preferably while still warm.

Serves 12

butter, for greasing
5 egg yolks, lightly beaten
1/2 cup superfine sugar (or the same quantity granulated sugar processed in a blender or food processor for 1 minute)
2 teaspoons cornstarch
1/2 cup whole milk
1 cup heavy cream
2-inch cinnamon stick
2 strips orange peel
1/2 teaspoon vanilla extract
13 ounces store-bought puff pastry
freshly grated nutmeg, for sprinkling
flour, for dusting

❁ Preheat the oven to 375°F. Lightly grease a 12-cup muffin pan. Combine the egg yolks and sugar in a mixing bowl. Stir in the cornstarch and mix to a smooth paste, then whisk in the milk.

❁ Heat the cream in a heavy saucepan until just starting to simmer but not boiling. Gradually whisk the hot cream into the egg mixture, then return the mixture to the pan. Add the cinnamon stick and orange peel. Whisk continuously over medium heat for about 5 minutes, until thickened. Immediately pour into a pitcher. Stir in the vanilla extract. Cover with plastic wrap to prevent a skin from forming and set aside.

❁ Place the sheet of puff pastry on a board and trim to a rectangle measuring about 11 x 9½ inches. Discard the trimmings or use in another recipe. Slice in half lengthwise to make two rectangles, each measuring 11 x 4¾ inches. Sprinkle one rectangle with freshly grated nutmeg. Place the other on top to make a sandwich. Roll up from the narrow end to make a log. Using a sharp knife, cut the log into twelve half-inch slices.

❁ Roll out the slices on a floured board to 4½-inch circles. Place the circles in the muffin-pan cups, lightly pressing down into the bottom and leaving a slightly thicker rim around the top edge.

❁ Remove the cinnamon stick and orange peel from the custard and discard. Pour the custard into the pastry shells.

❁ Bake for 20 minutes, or until the crust and filling are golden brown. Let the tarts cool in the pan for 5 minutes, then transfer to a wire rack to cool.

Scailtin (Milk Punch)

Ireland is famous for its dairy products and its whiskey. In this recipe, the two are combined in a hot, spicy punch that will warm the cockles of your heart.

Serves 2

2 cups whole milk
$\frac{1}{2}$ cup Irish whiskey
1–2 tablespoons honey, or to taste
$\frac{1}{8}$ teaspoon ground ginger
$\frac{1}{8}$ teaspoon ground cinnamon
freshly grated nutmeg, to decorate

- ❖ Pour the milk and whiskey into a small saucepan and stir in the honey, ginger, and cinnamon.

- ❖ Heat slowly, without letting the mixture boil, whisking briskly all the time to create a froth and to disperse the ground spices.

- ❖ Pour into two warm mugs and sprinkle with grated nutmeg.

ROCK OF CASHEL, COUNTY TIPPERARY

Whiskey & Orange Oat Cream Toddy

Hot, whiskey-spiked orange juice is topped with Ireland's favorite ingredients: thick cream and crunchy toasted oats. Serve it as a special nightcap on a chilly winter evening.

Serves 2

freshly squeezed juice of 6
 large oranges
1–1½ tablespoons honey, or to taste
½ cup heavy cream
3 tablespoons Irish whiskey
1½ tablespoons rolled oats, toasted

❁ Squeeze the juice from the oranges. There should be about 1½ cups.

❁ Strain the juice into a small saucepan. Add the honey and heat until hot but not boiling.

❁ Whip the cream lightly until soft peaks form. Stir in 1 tablespoon of the whiskey.

❁ Add the remaining 2 tablespoons of whiskey to the hot orange juice.

❁ Pour the mixture into 2 warm whiskey glasses. Top with a layer of whipped cream and sprinkle with toasted oats.

Index

apples
  Pickled Herring, Apple & Celery Salad 21
  Roast Goose with Apple Stuffing & Cider Gravy 51

bacon
  Bacon & Potato Cakes 68
  Bacon, Beet & Spinach Salad with Cashel Blue
    Cheese 28
  Dublin Coddle 38
  Red Cabbage with Mushrooms, Nuts & Bacon 66
  Scallop Chowder 15
barley
  Beef & Barley Broth 12
beef
  Beef & Barley Broth 12
  Beef & Stout Pies 46
beets
  Bacon, Beet & Spinach Salad with Cashel Blue
    Cheese 28
  Roasted Beet Packages with Horseradish Butter 54
black pudding
  Blood Sausage with Caramelized Pear and Cider 44
bread
  Boxty Bread 71
  Brown Soda Bread with Molasses 72
  Cockle & Mussel Gratin 34
  Irish Rarebit 27
  Molasses Bread 87
  Roasted Banana Shallots with Bread Crumbs &
    Cheddar 62
Buttered Kale with Chives & Lemon 65
buttermilk
  Irish Buttermilk Pancakes 10

cabbage
  Red Cabbage with Mushrooms, Nuts & Bacon 66
carrots
  Sticky Carrots with Whiskey & Ginger Glaze 56
celery
  Pickled Herring, Apple & Celery Salad 21
Champ 59
cheese
  Bacon, Beet & Spinach Salad with Cashel Blue
    Cheese 28
  Irish Rarebit 27
  Roasted Banana Shallots with Bread Crumbs &
    Cheddar 62
chicken
  Skink Soup 16
chives
  Buttered Kale with Chives & Lemon 65
Chocolate & Stout Ice Cream 78
cider
  Blood Sausage with Caramelized Pear and Cider 44
  Roast Goose with Apple Stuffing & Cider Gravy 51
  Sea Trout with Cider & Cream Sauce 32
Cockle & Mussel Gratin 34
crab
  Dublin Lawyer 37
  Irish Seafood Cocktail 18
cream
  Chocolate & Stout Ice Cream 78
  Irish Whiskey Trifle 76
  Oatmeal & Raspberry Cream 81
  Sea Trout with Cider & Cream Sauce 32
Currant Shortbread 88
custard
  Custard Tarts 90
  Irish Whiskey Trifle 76

dried fruit
  Currant Shortbread 88
  Irish Spiced Fruitcake 82
  Molasses Bread 87
  Porter Cake 84
Dublin Coddle 38
Dublin Lawyer 37

dumplings
  Slow-Roasted Shoulder of Lamb with Herb
    Dumplings 48

eggs
  Custard Tarts 90

fish
  Kipper & Potato Salad with Mustard Dressing 22
  Pickled Herring, Apple & Celery Salad 21
  Sea Trout with Cider & Cream Sauce 32
  Smoked Mackerel & Horseradish Pâté 24
Fruitcake, Irish Spiced 82

ginger
  Sticky Carrots with Whiskey &
    Ginger Glaze 56
goose
  Roast Goose with Apple Stuffing & Cider Gravy 51

Ham with Parsley Sauce 43
herbs
  Slow-Roasted Shoulder of Lamb with Herb
    Dumplings 48
herring
  Kipper & Potato Salad with Mustard Dressing 22
  Pickled Herring, Apple & Celery Salad 21
horseradish
  Roasted Beet Packages with Horseradish Butter 54
  Smoked Mackerel & Horseradish Pâté 24

ice cream
  Chocolate & Stout Ice Cream 78
Irish Buttermilk Pancakes 10
Irish Rarebit 27
Irish Seafood Cocktail 18
Irish Spiced Fruitcake 82
Irish Whiskey Trifle 76

kale
  Buttered Kale with Chives & Lemon 65
Kipper & Potato Salad with Mustard Dressing 22

lamb
  Slow-Roasted Shoulder of Lamb with Herb
    Dumplings 48
leeks
  Roasted Leeks with Parsley 60
lemons
  Buttered Kale with Chives & Lemon 65

mackerel
  Smoked Mackerel & Horseradish Pâté 24
Milk Punch 93
molasses
  Brown Soda Bread with Molasses 72
  Molasses Bread 87
mushrooms
  Beef & Stout Pies 46
  Red Cabbage with Mushrooms, Nuts & Bacon 66
mussels
  Cockle & Mussel Gratin 34
mustard
  Kipper & Potato Salad with Mustard Dressing 22

nuts
  Red Cabbage with Mushrooms, Nuts & Bacon 66

oats
  Bacon & Potato Cakes 68
  Oatmeal & Raspberry Cream 81
onions
  Roasted Banana Shallots with Bread Crumbs &
    Cheddar 62

parsley
  Ham with Parsley Sauce 43
  Roasted Leeks with Parsley 60
pears
  Blood Sausage with Caramelized Pear and Cider 44
Pickled Herring, Apple & Celery Salad 21
Pork Tenderloin with Roasted Rhubarb 40
Porter Cake 84
potatoes
  Bacon & Potato Cakes 68
  Boxty Bread 71
  Champ 59
  Dublin Coddle 38
  Kipper & Potato Salad with Mustard Dressing 22
  Scallop Chowder 15
prawns
  Irish Seafood Cocktail 18

raspberries
  Irish Whiskey Trifle 76
  Oatmeal & Raspberry Cream 81
Red Cabbage with Mushrooms, Nuts & Bacon 66
rhubarb
  Pork Tenderloin with Roasted Rhubarb 40
Roast Goose with Apple Stuffing & Cider Gravy 51
Roasted Banana Shallots with Bread Crumbs &
  Cheddar 62
Roasted Beet Packages with Horseradish Butter 54
Roasted Leeks with Parsley 60

sausage
  Blood Sausage with Caramelized Pear and Cider 44
  Dublin Coddle 38
scallions
  Champ 59
Scallop Chowder 15
Sea Trout with Cider & Cream Sauce 32
seafood
  Cockle & Mussel Gratin 34
  Irish Seafood Cocktail 18
  Scallop Chowder 15
Scailtin (Milk Punch) 93
shallots
  Roasted Banana Shallots with Bread Crumbs &
    Cheddar 62
Shortbread, Currant 88
Skink Soup 16
Slow-Roasted Shoulder of Lamb with Herb
  Dumplings 48
Smoked Mackerel & Horseradish Pâté 24
spices
  Irish Spiced Fruitcake 82
  Scailtin (Milk Punch) 93
spinach
  Bacon, Beet & Spinach Salad with Cashel Blue
    Cheese 28
Sticky Carrots with Whiskey & Ginger Glaze 56
stout
  Beef & Stout Pies 46
  Chocolate & Stout Ice Cream 78
  Porter Cake 84

trout
  Sea Trout with Cider & Cream Sauce 32

vegetables
  Skink Soup 16

whiskey
  Dublin Lawyer 37
  Irish Whiskey Trifle 76
  Oatmeal & Raspberry Cream 81
  Scailtin (Milk Punch) 93
  Sticky Carrots with Whiskey & Ginger Glaze 56
  Whiskey & Orange Oat Cream Toddy 94

THE
IRISH
PUB